Copyright © 20

All rights reserved. No part of this publication may be...,
transmitted in any form or by any means, including photocopying, recording, or other
electronic or mechanical methods, without the prior written permission of the publisher,
except in the case of brief quotations embodied in critical reviews and certain other
noncommercial uses permitted by copyright law. If you would like to purchase bulk or
wholesale copies, please contact the author at info@thebutterflyandthebully.com.

ISBN: 978-0-578-51971-5
www.thebutterflyandthebully.com

Front cover image by Lora Look
Bio picture by Anna Faiola
Book design by Joan Chizi
Illustrations by Lora Look

Thank you to 1st Book Club Publishing for providing the tools in order for me to
self-publish my first book.

1st Book Club Publishing
www.1stbookclub.com
P.O. Box 12161
St. Petersburg, FL 33733
Info@1stbookclub.com

"Transforming writers into Author-preneurs"

Disclaimer:

This book is for educational purposes only, and has been based on the views and
imagination of the author whether real or fictitious. The reader is responsible for his or
her own actions. Adherence to all applicable laws and regulations, including
international, federal, state and local governing professional licensing. business
practices, advertising, and all other aspects of doing business in the United States,
Canada or any other jurisdiction is the sole responsibility of the purchaser or reader.
Neither the authors nor the publisher assumes any responsibility or liability
whatsoever on behalf of the purchaser or reader of these materials.

ACKNOWLEDGEMENTS:

This book was inspired by my niece Rylei C. Heard and nephew Aston J. Morgan. I'd also like to dedicate this book to my beautiful nieces Mishyra Bailey and Raina Washington.

To my lost loved ones, ancestors and late brother George W. Morgan Jr., you are missed, loved, and respected.

Cheers to
Beautiful beginnings &
endings !!

"The Butterfly & the Bully"
Lola B. Morgan

TABLE OF CONTENTS

1. Characters and Enunciations
   - Rylei (Rye-lee)
   - Etana (Ee-tah-nuh)
   - Iya (Ee-yah)
   - Nkechi (En-Kay-Key)

2. Affirmation-a•fr•mei•shn the action or process of affirming something or being affirmed.

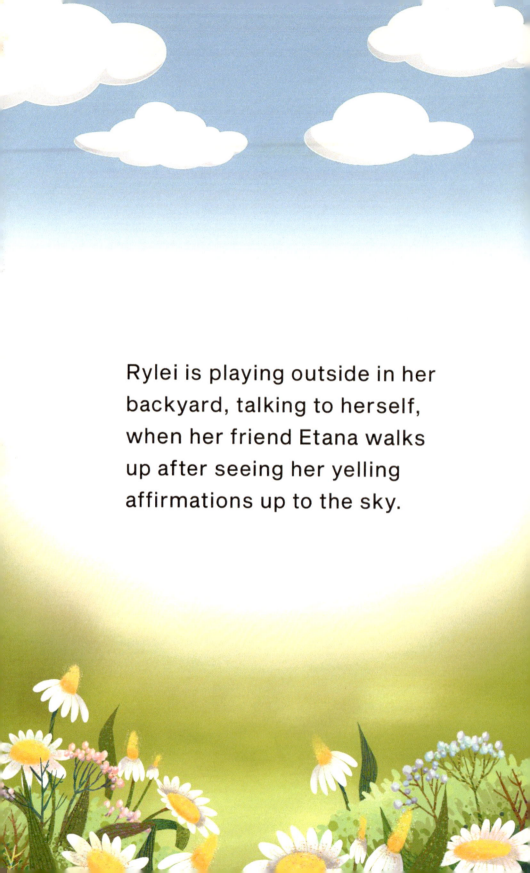

Rylei is playing outside in her backyard, talking to herself, when her friend Etana walks up after seeing her yelling affirmations up to the sky.

"I don't see what you see when you look at me," says Rylei.
"I AM AMAZING!
I AM STRONG!
I AM FIERCE!"
yells Rylei to the sky.

"In your eyes, there is only one version of me, but my world is colorful and limitless," says Rylei. "I'm just a girl making changes in the world. My heart is full, and I am running toward the sun."

Rylei begins to run! It's as if she is running away from the people who don't see her as AMAZING, STRONG, and FIERCE! What a beautiful girl she is—inside and out!

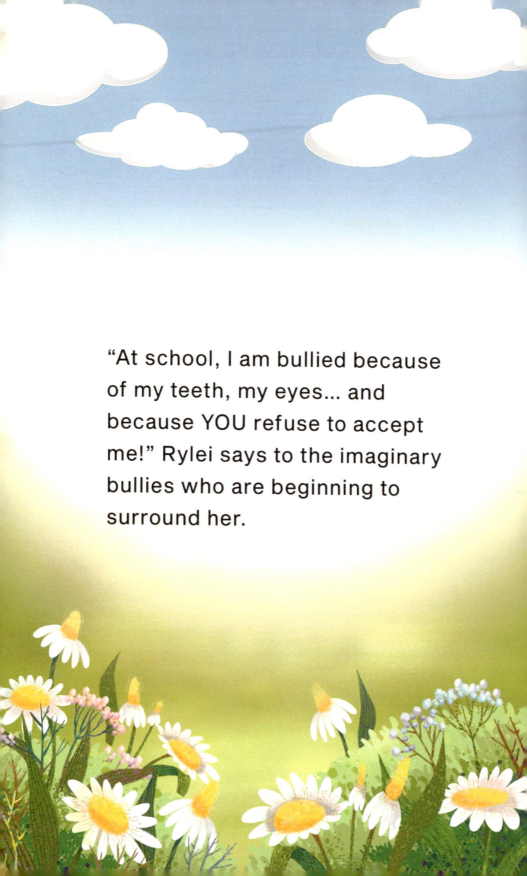

"At school, I am bullied because of my teeth, my eyes... and because YOU refuse to accept me!" Rylei says to the imaginary bullies who are beginning to surround her.

Rylei tells herself,
"I AM POWERFUL!"
"I AM A WARRIOR!"
"I AM A GODDESS!"
"God lives inside of me, and His spirit shines bright for the world to see. So why are you bothering me? Do you not see what I see when I look at me?" says Rylei to the imaginary bullies, who are teasing her and pulling at her hair.

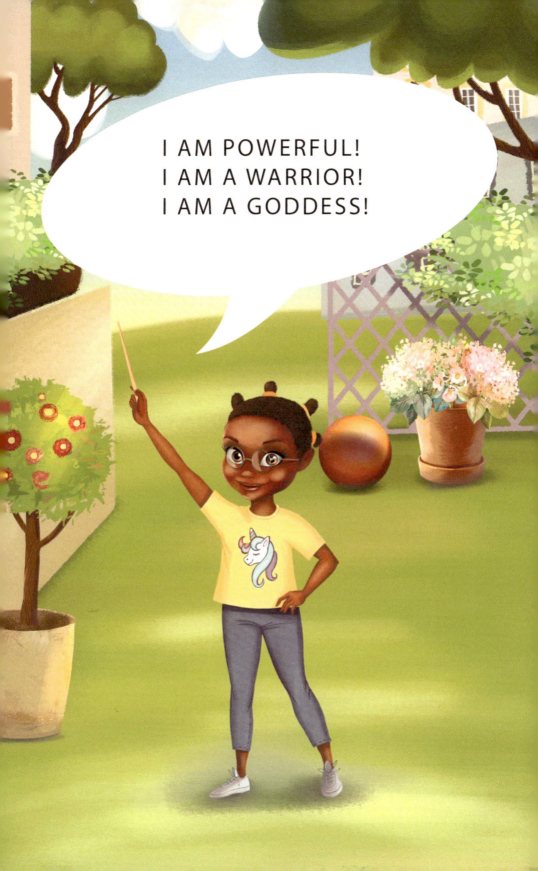

"Can you see me now? Because you're looking at me with a weird blank stare. My joy bothers you because you are sad. I just want to show you a new level of love." Rylei continues to speak to the imaginary bullies.

"My name is Rylei Angelou, and these are words from me to you. When I wave my magic wand, I can change into anything if I put my mind to it," says Rylei as her friend Etana Alicia walks up from behind.

Swoosh, swoosh,
I wish, I wish!

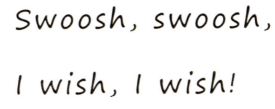

Rylei waves her wand and says, "Swoosh, swoosh, I wish, I wish... Mommy said to focus my mind on anything, so turn me into this!"
(As Rylei says this aloud to herself, she transforms into a butterfly!)

"Wooooah!" Etana Alicia exclaims excitedly, "HOW COOL! I wish I had SUPER-POWERS!" **(Rylei turns to Etana.)

"My wand isn't my super-power, my MIND is!" explains Rylei, who then turns back into a human.
**(Etana has a lightbulb moment!)

"So, you're telling me that anything I think I want to be, I can become?" asks Etana. "Yup! God blessed us with gifts, and it starts with our mind!" says Rylei. Rylei explains, "My Aunt Nkechi loves to tell me about how, before we were born, we chose our destinies.

Now we're simply on a journey, discovering the best version of ourselves!" The world is full of amazing things that make us happy, and, as long as we are good people, those amazing things will always follow us, like a magnet!

"We are all meant to tell our story and give back to the world. Some people get lost along the way but in our true heart and mind, we are able to find our purpose," says Rylei.

"I wish I had a story to tell," Etana sighs, looking down at the ground. "All I have is a sad story, and it makes me so mad at everyone! I used to be a good friend."

"But Etana, you are such a great person! Why have you been so angry lately? Some days you are so mean to me and the other kids," says Rylei.

"I'm sorry I've been mean. My dad passed away, and things just haven't been the same! Sometimes you all remind me of how happy he made me, and it just makes me really sad, and I don't know how to handle that," says Etana.

"I'm so sorry to hear that! What was his name? What do you remember most about him?" (Rylei)

"George! George Morgan! He was so awesome and super funny. Here in Chicago, I just see a lot of people dying, and it sucks to hear everyone else talk about their family when I only have my mom. Who's supposed to take me to the Father-Daughter Dance, my Uncle Jabari? I love him, but I want my DAD." (Whimpers) (Etana)

"Don't cry... When I'm sad, my dad tells me to pray. He says that speaking to God and my ancestors will help my heart feel better. Sometimes I draw or write in the journal my mom gave me, and it really helps!"

"Wait, I actually have an empty journal that you can use. Maybe it'll help you!" (Rylei pulls butterfly journal out of her bookbag)

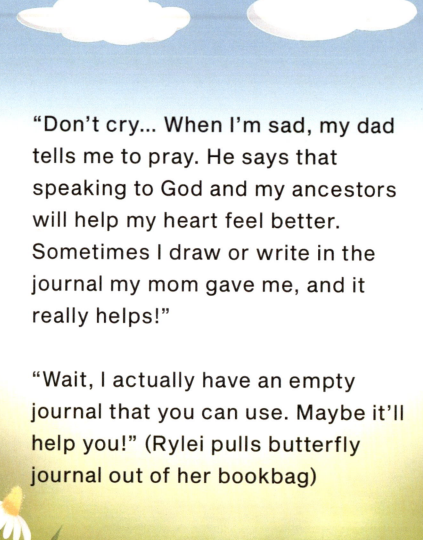

**It's beginning to get dark outside.

"I have to head home now, Rylei. Thank you so much for the gift!"

** They hug, and Etana goes home.

When Etana gets home, she sits at her kitchen table. Her mom Iya is cutting up some fruit for a before-dinner snack. Etana pulls out the butterfly journal that Rylei just gave to her. As she opens it up, her mind wanders to her memories of her father. She pulls out a pen and starts to write.

"Dear Dad, I miss you more than anyone knows. My heart hurts knowing you aren't here with me and Mommy! I'm so ANGRY! I never thought about how things would be without you."

"This is the WORST!" Etana bursts out with frustration!
Her mom turns around. "Sweetie, what's wrong?"
As Etana's eyes fill with tears, her mom comes close and sees Etana's letter. She quickly kneels down and holds her tight.

Iya begins to do breathing exercises with her. One, two, three... "Inhale, exhale. That's right, baby. Breathe in and out..." says Iya.

Iya sighs. "Now, I know this isn't easy for you. It's okay to feel the way you do. I miss your dad, too," Iya says. "Even though this is hard for both of us, we can help each other through this. I want you to know I will always be here for you."

"Mommy, I have something to tell you."(Etana)

"Okay. Is everything all right?" (Iya)

"Well, I've been kind of mean to the kids at school, especially my friend Rylei. After she gave me this cool journal, I realized how badly I'd been treating her. Do you think I was mean to her because Dad is gone?" (Etana)

"Maybe. But you should never let yourself be mean just because you're not feeling well inside." (Iya)

"I know, Mommy! The kids are always so happy and talking about their families, their dads, but I don't have one anymore. It's really hard to deal with." (Etana)

"Etana, you will always have a father. George will never stop being your father, and you have him and your ancestors in the heavens to always look over you." (Iya)

Iya rises to turn down the stove and sits next to Etana. "The next time you don't feel well inside, or you have a lot of thoughts you can't control, I want you to do this exercise." (Iya)

Etana looks up at her mom with excitement...

Iya takes the butterfly journal and writes:
"I am worthy, I am loved, I am grateful,
I am protected."

"Now, I want you to say this aloud.
We can do it together!" says Iya.

Together they repeat, "I am worthy,
I am loved, I am grateful, I am protected."

"Again," says Iya. They say it three times. (chants affirmations)
"Now, tell me, how do you feel?" (Iya)

"I feel better. My heart feels happier. Wow!" (Etana)
Iya smiles**

"Affirmations are like magic for your soul." (Iya tickles Etana, Etana giggles) "Anytime you feel frustrated, angry, alone, or upset, I want you to remember those four things: that you are worthy, loved, grateful, and protected. But you also must remember that other people also feel bad and get hurt in this world.

So what is it always up to us to do?" "Do nothing without intention," Etana says aloud as she points at the sign from the kitchen.

"That's my girl! Never forget that, baby. You are so special, and your father and I are very proud of you. Always remember who you are. Thank you for sharing that hard truth with me. I really appreciate it," says Iya.

Iya returns to the stove to finish dinner, humming happily.

Etana returns to her journal, feeling joyful and proud. As she continues to repeat her affirmations she then realizes that this is the start of something great for her!

"The Butterfly & the Bully"
Lola B. Morgan

Try these fun activities to help encourage positive powers in the mind!

AFFIRMATIONS
"I AM..."

Name:

Date:

Mood:

Affirmation:

For this exercise, I'd like you to list four things that describe you. Ex: "I am, GRATEFUL, FUN, HAPPY, HELPFUL".

AFFIRMATIONS "I AM..."

Name:

Date:

Mood:

Affirmation:

For this exercise, I'd like you to list four things that describe you. Ex: "I am, GRATEFUL, FUN, HAPPY, HELPFUL".

"GOOD THINGS ARE HAPPENING TO ME"

Name: Date:

Mood: Affirmation:

For this exercise, I'd like you to list four good things that happened this week.

"GOOD THINGS ARE HAPPENING TO ME"

Name:

Date:

Mood:

Affirmation:

For this exercise, I'd like you to list four good things that happened this week.

"DO NOTHING WITHOUT INTENTION"

Name:

Date:

Mood:

Affirmation:

For this exercise, I'd like you to list four things you will do to be kind to someone else. "Example, "I will bring my friend an apple for lunch because it's their favorite."

"DO NOTHING WITHOUT INTENTION"

Name: Date:

Mood: Affirmation:

For this exercise, I'd like you to list four things you will do to be kind to someone else. "Example, "I will bring my friend an apple for lunch because it's their favorite."

Author Bio:

Lola B. Morgan is a motivational enthusiast and an innate influencer within her community. Her magical aura captivates her audiences and is recognized by all whom she encounters.

Lola coaches those of all ages to help them live their life fearlessly through the art of manifestation! Inspired, Lola has poured her desires into writing. After losing her brother to gun-violence and noticing changes in today's society, Lola decided to write a children's book.

"The Butterfly & The Bully", is a creative tool that encourages youth to build healthier coping mechanisms caused by life stressors such as death, bullying, and trauma.

For coaching, speaking engagements, and book signing inquiries please visit: info@thebutterflyandthebully.com

"Securing the minds and confidence of people around the world—while bringing them to understand that their voice and character are relatable is essential in our growing process!" – Lola B. Morgan